T0158033

THE COLANTONIO SPORTS JOURNAL

THE COLANTONIO
SPORTS JOURNAL

Frederick Colantonio

THE COLANTONIO SPORTS JOURNAL

iUniverse books may be ordered through booksellers or by contacting:

iUniverse
1663 Liberty Drive
Bloomington, IN 47403
www.iuniverse.com
1-800-Authors (1-800-288-4677)

Because of the dynamic nature of the Internet, any web addresses or links contained in this book may have changed since publication and may no longer be valid. The views expressed in this work are solely those of the author and do not necessarily reflect the views of the publisher, and the publisher hereby disclaims any responsibility for them.

Any people depicted in stock imagery provided by Thinkstock are models, and such images are being used for illustrative purposes only. Certain stock imagery © Thinkstock.

ISBN: 978-1-4917-3425-4 (sc)
ISBN: 978-1-4917-3426-1 (e)

Print information available on the last page.

iUniverse rev. date: 12/01/2015

Dedication

THE COLANTONIO SPORTS JOURNAL is dedicated to my editor Emil Toth. He assisted me in drafting, editing and publishing my first book, *FREDERICK COLANTONIO 54 YEARS IN THE MEDIA* and has been wonderful in assisting me putting my articles and pictures together for this current book. Emil's positive attitude, faith and sense humor has been an inspiration to me. He is a gentleman and man with class.

I am also dedicating this book to my graphic designer, Katrina Zentefis. She was a tremendous help assembling, producing and printing my first issue of The Chicago Sports Journal. Had I not found her, I would have been totally lost. She has been also a great help to me in many areas. She works very hard and has excellent positive attitude, faith and sense humor. She is a mother with class as well.

ACKNOWLEDGEMENTS

I wish to thank a host of people, who published my feature articles in various Chicago community newspapers. They are too numerous to list. Other feature articles were published in a number of out of town newspapers. Unfortunately, through the years many of those newspapers have gone out of business and I have not been able to gather most of the articles I have written.

Special thanks to:

Ms. Rachel Gemo, Chief Executive Officer, at St. Benedict Preparatory School for giving me permission to reprint my articles in this book.

Brian Nadig, Publisher, at Nadig Newspapers, for giving me permission to reprint my articles in this book.

Elizabeth McManus, Managing Editor, of the Sauganash Sounds for allowing me to print my Restaurant Review article in this book.

Brian Nadig, Publisher of the Nadig Newspapers for allowing me to print my column, Sauganash Sampler, in this book.

Meryl Loop, Game Day Manager & Merchandise Manager, of the Wichita Wingnuts for permission to use the photo of the ballpark.

Pat Salvi, of the law firm Salvi, Schostok & Pritchard P.C. of Chicago and Waukegan, Illinois and Lindy Salvi, owners of the Schaumburg Boomers and Gary SouthShore RailCats,

Frederick Colantonio

professional baseball teams for giving me permission to use the photos of the ballparks.

Schostok & Pritchard P.C. for sending us photos of ball parks, which I have used in my newspaper.

Once again, I want to thank each and everyone of you for your co-operation from the bottom of my heart.

INTRODUCTION

The book you have in your hands is a small collection of the articles I have written recently for my own newspaper and community newspapers in my youth. Reporting sports news has been in my blood since I was a youngster.

My family moved from the west side to the northwest side of Chicago, I became interested in radio and in the journalism field while still in grade school. After school, I would rush home take out my tape recorder and do the play-by-play of the softball games of my classmates that played in the schoolyard. Growing up, I wrote brief reports, which were published in community newspapers in our area of Chicago. Compiling an article and having it published in the community newspapers gave me great pleasure.

At the same time, I was also interested in radio. If there were breaking stories or changes in sports scores, I would call the local radio stations and give them updates. When my first article was published in the community newspapers and my first sports update was accepted by the radio stations, I was hooked. All I wanted to be was a sports reporter on radio and in newspapers. My fascination with the field of reporting grew, and I was constantly in the library checking out books and reading articles in magazines about the broadcasting field.

Many of my years in grade school I sold newspapers at my newsstand on the corner of Keeler Ave and Irving Park Road. I made a few bucks. At the time, every cent I earned was well worth the effort. It was a great experience learning to sell, and it presented me with the opportunity to interact with people. I sold papers at my newsstand six days a week. On weekdays, I would be at my stand from 3 PM to 6 PM. On Saturdays, I would be there at 8 AM and leave at 6 PM.

During my high school years, I was more fascinated with radio than newspapers. I recall visiting the building that housed the WLS station. After my visit, I got off the elevator and saw a newsstand in the lobby of the main floor. There was a large variety of magazines and newspapers for sale. I took my time and looked at everything. I spotted a magazine labeled *Broadcasting*. I asked and was told it was sold every Monday. Every Saturday morning, I took the CTA train downtown to pick up a copy. I read every article in each magazine. I remember carrying either the broadcasting magazine and or the broadcasting yearbook around with me to all of my high school classes.

I knew I was headed for a career in sports reporting and journalism. It all began in those early days when I gave updates of the scores to the local radios stations. It was in my blood. I saw myself as a professional broadcaster and a newspaper journalist.

My career in sports broadcasting spanned nearly two decades, and I worked at over fifteen radio stations. Working at so many radio Stations, I decided it was time to aspire to something different. I followed my desire to be a radio-television columnist for a small suburban newspaper. My first attempt at being a journalist was with the Skokie Review.

In September, 1972, I felt there was a need for a radio-television column. With the increase of more AM FM broadcasting stations, I read nearly all of the suburban newspapers and there wasn't one radio-television columnist in any one of them. I called the Skokie Review and talked to the editor, Curt Thompson. Curt was very tall and slim and made you feel comfortable. He was the best editor I ever worked. He was efficient and knew his business. During the years between 1972 and 1980, I worked for four different editors. Curt was a very nice man and a loyal editor. I pitched my idea to Curt and after a minute of mulling it around in his head he told me he liked the idea of the column. I came up with the name of Hank Joyce for the column. The name, Hank, came from a television series and Joyce was my mother's maiden name. I had much more freedom and latitude using my new name. My new alias allowed me to get information about people who were going to be axed in the broadcasting field. I also was on the inside on knowing the changes of formats for radio stations. I never revealed my identity to any of the broadcasters I knew. The newspaper spelled Hank wrong. They spelled it Hanke. So everyone started pronouncing it like the handkerchief abbreviation, hankie. My column ran for eight years, from 1972 to 1980. It was also part of my job to drop the papers off at the newsstands where I got to know the customers. I definitely liked the job. I had made the transition from being a radio broadcaster to a newspaper journalist without having a college degree. I silenced all the naysayers who told me I needed a B.A. Degree in order to write. I proved them wrong and it gave me a great deal of satisfaction.

During my time at the Pickwick Newspapers, five editors and two managing editors came and went. The Pickwick Newspapers were later sold to the Pioneer Press Newspapers.

Over the years I wrote for a number of newspapers. I worked as a contributing reporter for Peacock Newspapers, Lerner Newspapers, Northcenter News, Passage Newspapers, Des Plaines Suburban Times, Niles Review, Sauganash Sounds, Chicago Post, City View, Des Moines, Iowa and Nadig Newspapers. I discovered writing a column did not provide the money I had imagined it would. The owner of the Nadig Newspapers was frugal with his money. He paid me five dollars for a column that he printed. I also delivered the papers and received forty percent commission on the sales. I kept building up my delivery business to the point where I had doubled the sales. Because I did so well, I asked for a higher commission. He refused to give it to me so I quit. For all of these papers, I was a contributing columnist, which meant that when I had an article of interest they would publish it in their paper.

Many of the newspapers I worked for were shut down for financial reasons, sold or merged with other publishing companies. The newspapers were also cutting back on the number of newspaper columns, interest stories and sports as well.

The main reason behind the demise of newspapers was the Internet. People could acquire the news on their computers. Many of the editors I knew found jobs in other professions or retired.

From October, 1986 to December, 2005, I published an advertising newspaper, The American Eagle Service Directory. I worked with local businesses and companies to promote their business cards. The ads ranged from 1/4 page to a full page. In 2010, I published the first edition of the Chicago Sports Journal, which is a quarterly newspaper. It has prospered since then and is still in operation.

While working at American Airlines, in the ramp tower, I came up with idea to start a Chicago sports newspaper on a quarterly basis. By the year 2010, I felt confident that I knew enough about the newspaper business and I struck out on my own and published my first quarterly sports newspaper, *The Chicago Sports Journal.*

The journal would include all sports from baseball to soccer. I endeavored to give each column unique names: From Hicks To Meyers for baseball, From Burdeen To Keefe in broadcasting field, From Dikita To Morris in football, From Langland to Romano in hockey. I am planning to add more columns in the near future.

Of course, like any other newspaper or retail business, initially, there were a few bugs to be worked out. It is the nature of most businesses in its startup stages.

I had no intention of putting the newspaper online at all. Every time I looked into the possibility, I found people in the computer business were either too busy or they went out of business after I spoke to them.

The paper's circulation started out at 8,000 and three years later, we started printing separate editions for downtown and northwest side businesses depending on the advertising. I decided to reduce the number of papers we printed to 6,000. The main reason was due to the number of professional and semi-professional sports teams in the Chicago area that were unable to sustain profitability and went out of business.

To help my own paper's profit margin, I began printing the name of the retail outlets where people could pick up copies of the newspaper. I did this to eliminate the need for the expensive newspaper boxes that dispense a paper when you supply the right amount of coins.

The 'At Your Service Column' has been a big success for the newspaper. This column informs our readers about specials and sales that retail businesses are having.

I've found that pictures of baseball stadiums we have placed in our issues were received very well. Our next goal is to give information and pictures of arenas and smaller stadiums.

Since the conception of the newspaper, I have been the sole owner. For a long while, I wrote every article in the paper. I am currently doing all the interviews myself. Now and then I have a guest columnist write an article of interest.

I am having the paper printed by a local printer that I came to know in my career as a reporter. I deliver the six thousand copies of the journal to the newsstands, hotels and businesses by walking. On the average, the paper contained eight pages.

There were a number of naysayers who expressed to me that my venture would never succeed. I know some of them were hoping I would fall flat on my face. They were people who did not take pleasure in anyone's success. They also did not take into account my passion and persistence. It took a great deal of time and effort, but I accomplished what I had set out to do. The newspaper is still in its infancy but I'm positive, in time, it will grow. I am confident it will, because I will help it grow and mature by nurturing it with hard work and determination.

Following is a sampling of the articles and advertisement that has appeared in my newspaper.

Frederick Colantonio

CHICAGO SPORTS JOURNAL

VOL. 3, ISSUE 4   DOWNTOWN EDITION   FALL 2013   FREE

Glad Cleaners

6412 N. Central Ave, Chicago
60645 · 1.773.631.1800 ·
www.gladcleaners.com

prime**bar**

155 N. Wacker Drive
Chicago, Il 60606
1.312.884.0000
primebarchicago.com

The Tech Edge
5355 W. Devon Ave
Chicago, Il 60646
1.773.345.8905
www.ttedge.net

FROM THE PUBLISHERS DESK...

Congratulations to Lindy and Pat Salvi, owners of the Gary Railcats and Schaumburg Boomers Baseball Teams. The Gary Railcats were the champions of the American Association and the Schaumburg Boomers who were the champions of the Frontier League for the 2013 baseball season.

We have added three more to our partnership. We now have 15 partners who are with us in helping our advertisers to promote their products and services.

CHICAGO SPORTS JOURNAL

CHICAGO SPORTS JOURNAL

VOL. 4, ISSUE 1 · SPRING/SUMMER 2014 · FREE

FROM THE PUBLISHERS DESK...

Welcome Everyone to Our Fourth Anniversary Issue of The Chicago Sports Journal

I had the pleasure of watching a Triple A ball last Wednesday in New Orleans. Iowa Cub pitcher Chris Rusin pitch a no hit ball game against the New Orleans Zephyrs. It was the first no hitter thrown in 30 years by Iowa Cub pitcher. The last time a no hitter was thrown by Iowa Cub pitcher Reggie Patterson on August 21, 1984 with a 2-0 victory over the Omaha Royals.

CHICAGO SPORTS JOURNAL

Frederick Colantonio

FROM THE PUBLISHERS DESK...

Welcome to our fifth anniversary edition to the Chicago Sports Journal. I want to thank very much my graphic designer Katrina Zentefis who has been a big help to me and the employees at the John Swift Print Company in Buffalo Grove, Illinois.

World's Largest Block Party on Saturday June 27, 2015. For more information, www.oldstpats.org.

Congratulations to Jon Larson, General Manager at the Prime Bar on his promotion as Director of Operations for Restaurant-America

which owns and operations The Prime Bar. Erin Kowalski, Assistant General Manager at The Prime bar, has been named General Manager replacing Jon Larson. Erin worked very hard moving up thru the ranks. Congrats to you both.

Check out the historical sports t-shirts at Atlas Stationers, Inc, 217 W. Lake Street in Chicago. (312) 726-5261... They historical t-shirts of the Chicago Whales baseball, Chi American Hockey, Chicago Flyers basketball, Chicago Rockets football, Chicago Hornets and a lot more historical sports t-shirts.

CHICAGO SPORTS JOURNAL

CHICAGO SPORTS JOURNAL

THE COLANTONIO REPORT
(MINOR LEAGUE BASEBALL RATINGS)

The top 15 teams based on wins, loses and winning pctg as follows on June 13, 2012:

1. Akron Aeros AA Eastern League
2. Omaha STrom Chasers AAA P.C.L.
   Sacramento River Cats AAA P.C.L.
4. Pawtucket Red sox AAA International League
   Fresno Grizzlies AAA P.C.L.
6. Tigres de Quintana Roo AAA Mexican League

7. Jackson Generals AA Southern League
8. Sultanes de Monterrey AAA Mexican League
   Reno Aces AAA P.C.L.
10. Frisco Rough Riders AA Texas League
11. Olmecas de Tabasco AAA Mexican League
12. Oklahoma City Redhawks AAA P.C.L.
13. Trenton Thunder AA Eastern League
14. Indianapolis Indians AAA International League
15. Charlotte Knights AAA International League

SPORTS BRIEFS

By Fred Colantonio

The **Biloxi Shuckers** of the Southern Baseball League have announced they will played 15 home games in Huntsville this 2015 season. They operated as the Huntsville Stars last season. the Biloxi Shuckers baseball stadium is expected not to be ready until sometime in June of this year.

****

The **Fresno Grizzlies** of the Pacific Coast Baseball League will play one game as Fresno Raisin Eaters during the 2015 season.

The **Independent Basketball Assn** has announced for the upcoming season they would include seven full schedule team and two partial-schedule teams, or branding teams coming up this season. They will have a total of eight teams.

****

Southern Professional Hockey League will have new team called Macon Mayhem for the 2015-2016 upcoming season. The team was formerly known as Augusta (GA) Riverhawks which was forced to sit out the 2013-1014 season.

The **Beloit Snappers** have a new radio station outlet in 2015. They will have 40 home games broadcast throughout the season on JCR, 103.5 FM, as well as streaming live on the internet. The games will by the host of JCR's Wisconsin Sports Report - David Krapf.

****

The **International Baseball League**: The Pawtucket (RI) Red Sox team, also known as the PawSox, of the Triple-A International League has been sold and new ownership plans to make a move on the team and proposed new stadium nearby Providence (RI) for the 2017 baseball season.

****

The new **East Coast Baseball League** team announced for Old Orchard Beach (ME) will be called the Old Orchard Beach Surge when the independent league starts its inaugural season this year. The league plans to have six teams. One of the teams will be a traveling team.

****

The **American Hockey League** has announced a new 2015-2016 Bakersfield team, which is currently operating as the Oklahoma City Barons, the team will be called the Bakersfield Condors when it becomes part of the league's new five team Pacific Division next season

SPORTS BRIEFS

By Fred Colantonio

Tune in "The Sports Corner" heard ever Saturday from 8am to 10am on WRLR(FM) Round Lake, Illinois on 98.3 FM dial. With host Rusty Stabler and Pat Cameron. This will mark their fifth anniversary on the radio station. Keep up the good work Pat and Rusty. Also, special guest star on "The Sports Corner," is Kevin Horan. Check it out the Sports Corner. They have the up-to-date minute in professional football, basketball, hockey and other sports.

****

Speak of Kevin Horan, Kevin Horan's website www.kevinhoranrankings.com has now expanded on radio station WJDS(FM) 87-9 on Friday's at 12 noon and also on the Great Lakes Radio Network on Thursday's at 1pm. For more information check out www.kevinhoranrankings.com.

****

The Schaumburg Boomers Baseball Club has announced the re-signing of manager Jamie Bennett for the 2013 season. The Boomers ended up with a 54-42 record baseball season in 2012.

****

The Continental Football League has announced a new member of the league...The Kane County Dawgs. It looks like - they are replacing the Chicago Pythons who won't return to the league. Also, the Indianapolis Enforcers won't return to the league.

The Mc Henry K-Niners Baseball Club which was suppose to be in the Frontier League are currently still under construction with the stadium and other issues.

****

Former Chicago Cub farmhand outfielder Nic Jackson of the Fargo-Moorhead Redhawks has been named the Pointstreak American Association "Star of Stars" for the 2012 season, the league office announced recently.

****

The Kane County Cougars recently announced a two year working agreement player development contract (PDC) with the Chicago Cubs.

****

Former Chicago Cubs manager Jim Riggleman has been named triple-a manager of the Cincinnati Reds farm team, Louisville Bats. Jim also managed the San Diego Padres and Washington Nationals of the National League.

****

The Chicago Cubs have announced they have appointed Mark Johnson manager of their Midwest League baseball team the Kane County Cougars and the Joliet Slammers have announced the appointment of Chris Franklin as General Manager.

SPORTS BRIEFS

By Fred Colantonio

Check out the website www.monsterjam.com. It is awesome website! By the way, our Chicago's own Jay Polena will be in monster jam. Starting next month in the first quarter, he will be on the road in Columbus, Ohio on January 4-5 at Nation Wide; January 12-13 in Wichita, Kansas at Instrut Bank Arena; January 18-19 in Milwaukee, Wisconsin at the Bradley Center;

January 25-26 in Louisville, Ky at Freedom Hall; February 1-2 in Rockford, Il Harris Bank Center; February 8-9-10 in Rosemont, Il at All State Arena; February 15-16 in Cleveland, Ohio and on March 2nd in Detroit, MI at Ford Field. If you would like to meet Jay, visit him at his business PennyPincher Resale Shop at 4804 N. Central Ave in Chicago.

That's it in sports briefs everyone and drive with care.

The Colantonio Sports Journal

SPORTS BRIEFS

By Fred Colantonio

Appalachian Baseball League announced that the Pulaski (Va) Mariners rookie level team will not be returning in 2015.....Prospect League the summer-collegiate plans to expand to 12 teams next season with Kokomo (In)......East Coast Baseball League, a new professional independent is trying to organize with teams in Ontario (Canada), New York, New Jersey, Pennsylvania, Michigan, Ohio and Indiana.....United Baseball League has announced the San Angelo Colts of the independent league have filed for bankruptcy protection to prevent foreclosure on their home stadium.

Eastern League; Plans to build a new stadium in downtown Hartford (Ct) for the relocated New Britain Rock Cats of the Double-A Eastern league are facing opposition.....The Schaumburg Boomers Baseball team of the Frontier League have announced hitting coach C.J. Thieleke was named coach of the year and Mike Tlusty was named groundkeeper of the year in the Frontier League. Great job done by the Schaumburg Boomers baseball club.

St. Viator in Arlington Heights has a new basketball coach, Quin Hayes. Quin was named to the position on August 20th.....Title Boxing Club announced they have opened their 100th club location in Fishers, Indiana. The club is owned by Dan Hannay. Dan owns another Title Boxing Club down

in Indianapolis, Indiana.....There is a Title Boxing Club here in Chicago. The Title Boxing Club is located at 2417 N. Clark Street in Chicago. You can reach them at 1.773.312.4726, www.titleboxingclub.com.

Kevin Horan Rankings for college football the top 10
1. Penn State
2. Mississippi
3. Oklahoma
4. Boston College
5. Texas A&M
6. BYU
7. Notre Dame
8. Pittsburgh
9. USC
10. Alabama

The Chicago Cubs have announced two year agreement with their Triple A farm team the Iowa Cubs. Awesome Iowa Cubs. Keep up the good work.

The Schaumburg Boomers Baseball Team won their second championship in a row in the Frontier Baseball League. They are the third team that has done it.

SPORTS BRIEFS

By Fred Colantonio

Here are some sports talk program heard on educational radio stations thru out Chicagoland. WCRX(FM) 88.1 Bench Warmer Sports talk heard every Tuesday from 7:00-9:00 pm and on Saturday, Nothin But Net from 7:00 to 9:00 am... WLTL(FM) 88.1 TPH (Sports) heard on Tuesday's from 7:00-8:00 pm and TNT (sportstalk) 8:00-10:00pm on Thursday.

WHPK(FM) 88.5... The ALL Sports alternating with Gospel in the streets of Chicago from 12 noon to 1:00 pm on Thursday... WLUW(FM) 88.7 Sunday Sports Shootout with Darrel D heard at 11:00 am to 12 noon... WIIT(FM) 88.9 Sportstalk heard on Wednesday from 2:00 to 4:00 pm... The Sports KIngs Talk Show with Gene Thompson heard on Saturday from 10:00 pm to 12 midnight.

You can listen to 24 hours sports talk shows on The Score - WSCR(AM) 670 and WMVP(AM) 1000 ESPN.

The Normal Cornbelters have renew the contract of their manager Brooks Carey for the 2014 season coming up... Windy City Thunderbolts are preparing their roster for the 2014 season coming up... The Frontier League will open the season on May 16, 2014... Another new Chicago area football team has been announced recently. The are called the Chicago Assassins of the American Indoor Football League...

****

Check out Chicagoland Performer Jay Polena #48 of Monster Jam. He will be appearing Jan3-4 Columbus; Jan 10-11 in Evansville; Jan 31-Feb 1 in Fargo; Feb 7-9 at Rosemont, Il; Feb 14-16 Cleveland, Ohio; Mar 7-9 Toledo; Mar 14-16 in grand Rapids, Michigan.

SPORTS BRIEFS

Jay Polena, performer in Monster Jam and owner of Penny Pinchers Resale Shop here in Chicago, has announcer is schedule coming up. June 21-22 in Erie, Pa; Aug 2-3 New Orleans; Sept 28-29 Arnhem, Holland; Oct 19 Sydney, Australia; Nov 2-3 Helsinki, Finland and Nov 9 in Stockholm, Sweden.....

****

The basketball merger between the Independent Basketball Association and Premier Basketball League has come to halt. Both leagues will go their own coming up in the next season. IBA Standings as follows: 1) Kankakee County Soldiers 12-3; 2) Gary Splash 9-6; 3) Kenosha Ballers 7-7; 4) Chicago Redline 7-8; 5) St. Louis Trotters 4-9; 6) Lansing Capitals 3-10 7) Lake Michigan Admirals 2-10.

IBA Branding Teams Standings as follows: 1. New Jersey G-Force 2-0; 2) Springfield Xpress 5-7; 3) Albany Legends 0-2; 4) Lake County Stars 0-6.

****

Kevin Horan Rankings College Baseball this will be the last ranking until after the college World Series.

1. Vanderbilt
2. LSU
3. North Carolina
4. Virginia
5. Louisville
6. Bryant
7. Campbell
8. Austin Peay
9. CS-Fullerton
10. Oregon State

SPORTS BRIEFS

By Fred Colantonio

The Chicago Wolves Hockey Team of the AHL are getting ready for the play-offs. Get your tickets now by calling 1-800-the wolves or by visiting ChicagoWolves.com game on either XFinity CN100, MY50, or The U Too (26.2).

If you have any questions regarding the Chicago Wolves, call their Director of Public relations Lindsey Willhite at 1.847.832.1964. You send him email at lwillhite@chicagowolves.com today.

****

Check out www.monsterjam.com - Chicago's own performer Jay Polena will be performing in monster jam in Green Bay on April 6-7; Moline on April 27-28 and in Erie, Pa on June 21-22. For more details, visit www.monsterjam.com today.

****

Listen to Sports Corner on radio station WRLR(FM) 98.3 IN Round Lake, Illinois. With your hosts Pat and Rusty. Giving away Chicago Wolves hockey tickets and a lot more. They are on the air from 8 to 10 am on Saturday's.

BASEBALL NOTES

There are a lot of changes in minor league baseball this year. That includes the independent leagues. The Schaumburg Flyers will not play this year. They were hoping to be a traveling team and that did not work out either. They are still looking for a new owner and still owe money to the Village of Schaumburg.

The **Kalamazoo Kings** of the Frontier League will also go dark this year. Kalamazoo Kings president and majority owner Bill Wright said the organization will go dark for the 2011 season. During the fall the team was up for sale. The Frontier League has agreed to give the Kings a one year release to decide what they can do. I am myself was trying to get in touch with Bill Wright and it is hard to do.

The **Rockford Riverhawks** formerly with the Northern League and a member of the new North American League, have announced plans they will league the NAL and join the Frontier League for the 2011 season. The Rockford Riverhawks also announced their new manager for the 2011 season. Rick Austin has been named manager. Patrick O'Sullivan hitting coach and Scott Roehl pitching coach.

Southwestern States League: The league which planned to start play this spring with five baseball teams called the Blackwell(OK) Broncos, Brenham(TX) Bulls, Clovis(NM) Rhythm, Elk City (OK) Wranglers, and Kingfisher (OK) Pioneers, has apparently shut down operations.

The **Atlantic Baseball League:** A group wanting to place an ABL franchise in Frederick (MD) is prepairing to make a bid for a lease on the city's ballpark for 2012 season.

The **Ultimate Baseball League:** The proposed UBL awhich was planning to start its inaugural season in 2011 with four teams playing a 35-game season, has decided to push back its start until 2012.

As **Yuma Scorpions** general manager Jose Melendez announced new player-manager Jose Canseco at the press conference recently, a familiar figure walked into the room. Ozzie Canseco, who will for his brother and also be his bench coach for the 2011 season.

The **Windy City Thunderbolts** have announced their new hitting coach for the 2011 season, and the name is very popular on the south side of Chicago and in Crestwood. Brent Bowers, who managed the team in the 2005 and 2006 season.

Gary SouthShore RailCats have hired Tim Calderwood for the 2011 season as its play-by-play announcer. Tim, was the 2009 Frontier League Broadcaster of the Year. We wish him the best this season.

FROM BURDEEN TO KEEFE

Welcome to the Chicago Sports Journal radio column. It will take time to grow and word of mouth will get around as well.

Donna Mullen a veteran broadcast journalist who has been around. Was recently filling on the True Oldies Channel - WLS-FM (94.7). I must say, Donna Mullen sounded awesome. Keep up the good work Donna.

-υ-

WLUP (FM) has announced the newest "LOOP ROCK GIRL." Her name is Tricia Van Der Slik. Although for the next year, she will be known as 'LOOP ROCK GIRL TRICIA.'

-υ-

Weigel Broadcasting announced new management promotions and hires at their station.

Norman Shapiro, President of Chicago based Weigel Broadcasting Company, has announced three company leadership recently.

Neil Sabin who was recently Executive Vice-President of Weigel, has been promoted President of Content and Networks for Weigel Broadcasting.

John Hendricks will become Weigel Broadcasting's Executive Vice-President of Sales.

Robert Ramsey will become Weigel's Vice-President/General Manager of WCIU-TV in Chicago.

Word is out that radio station WRTE (FM) known as RADIO ARTE 90.5 - might be for sale. The National Museum of Mexican Arts (NMMA) purchased WCYC-FM in 1996 from Boys/Girls Club of Chicago. Call letters were changed in 1997.

-0-

Lisa Greene formerly with WILV(FM) 100.3 AND FRESH (105.9), is currently with WCPT (am 820, "Chicago's Progressive Talk.").

Lisa Greene does on-air, voicetracks, imaging commerical VO, writing projects, on-camera work. If you would like to contact Lisa Greene, check her website out at www.lisagreene.com

She does excellent job.

-0-

For the latest information on your traffic reports from roadblocks to construction on the expressways. Get the up to date from Christina Filiaggi on WLS-AM 890 am on the "Roe Conn Show." from 2:00 - 6:00 pm Monday through Friday.

-0-

Bruce Wolf & Dan Proft Show is heard weekends on WLS-AM 890. 12 NOON to 3:00 pm on Saturday's and Sunday's from 1:00 - 3:00 pm.

BASEBALL PARKS

Billings Montana Mustangs Stadium

Gary Indiana South Shore Railcats Stadium

Schaumberg Illinois Boomers Stadium

South Bend Four Winds Field at Covoleski Stadium

Wichita Kansas Wingnuts Stadium

I've had the opportunity to attend dozens and dozens of baseball games in stadiums across the country and provide reports to various newspapers but have not been able to receive permission to print photos of the ballparks prior to the printing of this book.

Frederick Colantonio

CHICAGO SPORTS JOURNAL

THE COUNTY BAR

Chopped Chicken Salad $7.99

Fountain Drinks, Pepsi, Diet Pepsi, Sierra Mist, Mountain Dew and Orange Crush for $1.99 and $2.99.

The Burger Joint Chicago is open from Mon-Thur 11am to 3pm and Fri & Sat 11am to 5 am. They deliver. 1.312.440.8600.

****

The Buddy Guy's Legends, 700 S. Wabash Ave in Chicago - has appetizers you would like. Try the Southern Fried Okra with basket of okra served with honey mustard and sauce for $6.

Also, Catfish Tenders for $10 - strips of Mississippi Catfish served with Cajun tartar sauce.

For desserts, try the Big Drunken Chocolate cake for only $10

Give them a call at 1.312.427.1189.

Note: Menu and prices change at times.

The Prime Bar, 155 N. Wacker Drive in Chicago, had a promotion going on. It's called "Warm Weather Cold Drinks." Thursday & Friday Specials, Thursday $4 Chi-Town Brews excludes matilda revolution and Friday $5 glasses or $30 bottles of Select Wine.

Try the Prime Bar "Scottish Salmon." - pan roasted lemon dill compound butter, roasted vegetable pearl couscous, Citrus baby greens. 17 -

Also, "Baked Mac & Cheese." - four cheese blend, roasted tomato 11 - add cheese 15 - add shrimp 16 and add lobster 17.

The Prime Bar also has gift cards for you. For more information stop in at The Prime Bar or go online PrimeBarChicago.com. Call them at 1.312.884.0000.

****

Burger Joint Chicago, 675 N. Franklin Street in Chicago - has a good choice of food and drinks for your selection. Milk Shakes (Vanilla, Chocolate and Strawberry) $2.99

Chili Dog with Merkts Cheddar, Onion for $2.99....Hot Dog with tomato, onion, pickle, mustard, relish, sport peppers, celery salt for only $2.79.

By Fred Colantonio

The Prime Bar, located at 155 N. Wacker Drive in Chicago, has daily and weekly specials. (Specialties) bento box lunch only, ask server for daily special $14.99.....omelette du jour chef's selection $12.99.....(Small Plates) buffalo chicken tenders $7.99 smoked onion ranch.....spinach & pepper jack queso dip $9.99 tortilla chips.....Call them today at 1.312.884.0000

****

The Burger Joint Chicago, 675 N. Franklin Street in Chicago, Check out their meals. #1 Hamburger with lettuce, tomato, onion, pickle ketchup Regular $8.99 * Large $9.99 * Double +$1.50.....#7 Italian Beef with Mozzarella Giardiniera - Regular $8.99 * Large $9.99.....Fountain Drinks $1.99/$2.99. Call Denny at 1.312.440.8600

****

Buddy's Guy Legend, 700 S. Wabash Ave in Chicago, has live blue nightly. Check the groups out. Lunch menu - served from 11am-4pm. Free live acoustic lunch time sets every Monday-Friday 12pm-2pm.

Catfish tenders $10.00 - strips of Mississippi Catfish served with cajum tartar sauce.....Blackened Bourbon Shrimp $11.00 - blackened jumbo shrimp shrimp flambeeds in a spicy bourbon sauce.....Gumbo - Cup $5.00, Bowl $8.00 Andouille sausage and Tasso ham served with cornbread - cup or bowl

Check out the excellent desserts - Peanut Buddy Pie $6.00

Call today at 1.312.427.1190

****

Prices and menus change on a daily or weekly basis.

Prime Bar - www.restaurant-america.com

Burger Joint Chicago - www.burgerjointchicago.com

Buddy Guy's Legend - www.buddyguy.com

If you would like to make a reservation to any the places we mention, give them call at their phone number today.

THE COUNTRY BAR

Burger Joint is located in Oglivie Transportation Center on Canal and Madison Street in Chicago. They have Specialty Fries: Chili Cheese Fries and Blue Cheese Fries for $3.99 and Fresh Cut Fries for $1.99/$3.99.....Try the Wild Cowboy with sliced cheddar, bacon, bbq....Texas Thunder Ribs....half slab ribs for $12.99 and full slap ribs for $20.99. Specialty Burgers $7.99. Add American cheese for only 60 cents...upgrade to a regular meal for +$3 or larger for +$4. They have choose of cold drinks and beers also for your choose.

****

Edens The Original, 6045 N. Cicero Ave, Chicago offers a variety of breakfast, lunch, dinner and more. Try the breakfast express - 2 eggs any style with bacon, sausage patties or ham for only $5.85.....Butter-milk Pancakes (3 stack) for only $4.45 and also French toast for $4.45.

(Pure Beef Viennas) Condiments; Mustard, Relish, Onion, Pickle &Tomato. Hot Dog $2.75; Cheese Dog $3.35; Jumbo Hot Dog $3.65 and Polish Sausage $4.25..........

(100% Beef Burgers) all burgers are topped with; mayo, mustard, ketchup, lettuce, tomato, pickle & onions. Beef Burgers $3.75....Double Burger $4.75.....Cheeseburger $3.95...Bacon Cheeseburger $4.85

They also have cold sandwiches, dinner specials, cold drinks, coffee and a lot more to choose from. Give them a call at 1.773.736.3385....check out their website at http://www.edensfast-food.com/

CHICAGO SPORTS JOURNAL

By Fred Colantonio

The Prime Bar, located at 155 N. Wacker Drive in Chicago, has daily and weekly specials. They have sliders - served on toasted min-buns with fried onion strings - prime rib $9.99 ***** hamburger lettuce, tomato, red onion, pickles, pretzel bun $9.99 w/cheese $10.99 **** California chicken guacamole, shredded romaine, plum tomatoes, julienne cucumbers, fantina cheese, whole wheat kaiser roll $10.99. Give them call at 1.312.884.0000. Ask for Melissa Santiago the General Manager. www.restaurant-america.com

****

Buddy's Guy Legends, 700 S.Wabash Ave. in Chicago, has live blue nightly. Check the groups out. They have lunch special like Southern Fried Okra served basket of okra with hone-mustard sauce for $6.00 ***** Fried Oysters basket of cornmeal breaded oysters served with Cajun cocktail sauce for only $10.00 ***** Highway 61 Caesar Salad romaine lettuce with cherry tomatoes, red onions, caesar dressing, cornbread croutons, and parmesan cheese - Small $5.00 & Large $8.00 - Desert special **** Key Lime Pie $6.00

****

The Burger Joint Chicago, 675 N. Franklin in Chicago, check out the #2 Gyros with cucumber sauce, tomato, onion for a regular size for only $8.99 and a large for $9.99.........Also, #6 Polish with grilled onions and mustard for a regular size for $6.99 and a large for $7.99...They have vanilla, chocolate and strawberry milkshakes for $2.99....Stop in and see Denny for more details. Call 312.440.8600

****

The Moher Public House, 5310 W. Devon Ave. in Chicago, have weekly specials dine only. On Monday's, $5.00 Moher Burger with purchase of a beverage - extra $1.00 - substitutions: $1.00 and on Tuesday's, try $5.00 Well Martinis * $7.00 your call, $1.00 off all drafts and $5.00 quesadilla and finally, Wednesday's half-price bottles of wine $2.00 off flatbreads. Call the Moher Public House at 1.773.467.1954

****

If you would like to make a reservation to any the places we mention, give them call at their phone number today.

THE COUNTRY BAR

The Prime Bar, 155 N. Wacker Drive in Chicago (between Lake and Randolph Streets), excellent lunch menu. Roasted Red Pepper Hummus; Cucumber, kalamata olive relish toasted flatbread; Tomato & Basil Flatbread; Mozzarella, Roasted Garlic; Cheddar Biscuits; Bacon maple butter and fruit preserve; Beer Mussels; Caramelized shallots, hefeweizen cilantro broth, toasted garlic bread; Primebar burger; goat cheese, arugula, mushrooms, grilled tomato, caramelized onion, pickles, pretzel bun. You have a choose of wines, beers, deserts and a lot more. For your parties, meetings, and a lot more, contact them at 1.312.884.0000. Ask for Jon Larson the General Manager and Erin Kowalski, Assistant General Manager.

****

Local Mocha Café, 8836 Brookfield Ave in Brookfield, Illinois. They have awesome choose of warm/cold drinks, coffee, chai teas, lattes, espressos, hot chocolate. they have bagels. muffins, cookies, fruits and snacks. Also, house specialties and fruit smoothies. Open Mon-Fri from 5am to 6pm, Sat 6am to 3pm and Sun 7am to 3pm. Give them a call at 1.708.485.7990. Check out their website at http://www.locamochacoffee.com/ They are right across the street from the Metra train station.

****

Weber Grill Restaurant, 539 N. State Street in Chicago, offers a variety for lunch menu. They have a variety to choose from. Excellent burgers, pizzas, entrée salads. Dinner, try their steaks, fish, even salads firecooked on Weber Grills by the grill experts. They have kid menu; wine list, bar bites and a lot more. For your next reservation, stop in and see Melissa Santiago, the Assistant General Manager, or email her at msantiago@thewebergrill.com. Call today at 1.312.467.9696 or fax them at 1.312.467.0536.

****

By Fred Colantonio

My mornings usually start with a cup of coffee with a sweet roll, donuts or a slice of coffee cake. But when the weather outside is cold, there's something special about settling inside with something warm in your hands and seat back with your laptop, Iphone or Ipad and just go through your emails or your txt messages and relax with your favorite drink.

Edens The Original, 6045 N. Cicero Ave in Chicago, offers a variety of breakfast, lunch, dinner and more. try the breakfast express - 2 eggs any style with bacon, sausage patties or ham for only $5.95. Buttermilk pancakes (3 stack) for only $4.45 and also French toast for $4.45.

(Pure Beef Viennas) Condiments; Mustard, Relish, Onion, Pickle & Tomato. Hot Dog $2.75; Cheese Dog $3.35; Jumbo Hot Dog $3.65 and Polish Sausage $4.45.

(100% Beef Burgers) all burgers are topped with mayo, mustard, ketchup, lettuce, tomato, pickle & onions. Beef Burgers $3.75....Double Burger $4.75.....Cheeseburger $3.95......Bacon Cheeseburger $4.85

They also have cold sandwiches, dinner specials, cold drinks, coffee and a lot more to choose from. Give them a call at (773) 736-3385.... check out their website at http://www.edensfastfood.com/

Edens Fast Food - (773) 736-3385 - Great Food - Great Value - Chicago, IL. 60645

****

Weber Grill, 539 N. State Street in Chicago, offers a variety of breakfast, lunch and dinner. Try the breakfast menu of French Toast and let me tell you - it is awesome with bacon and fruit salad. You can't go

...rough. They also have pancakes and other breakfast menu. For lunch, try the Classic Burger, pizzas and other entrée salads. Dinner, the steaks are out of this world with a bake potato with butter. They also have kids menu and outstanding wine list for your pleasure. Call today at (312) 467.9696.

****

The Prime Bar, 155 N. Wacker Drive in Chicago has some special ties... bento box ask your service for today's lunch special. They have good salads and I must admit, I love salads with ranch dressing... braised short ribs - asiago polenta, crispy brussel sprouts, tobacco onion strings, au jus $29... spicy rigatoni & sausage... smoked sausage, spinach, parmesan, basil, rustic san marzano tomato sauce $19... If you are a cheese lover, try the mac & cheese... four cheese blend, jalapeno, bacon $12, with bbq chicken 15 with shrimp $19... Try bacon cheeseburger with lettuce, tomato and pickles $11.

****

Monk's Pub, 205 W, Lake Street in Chicago (Lake Street & Wells) opens at 10 am. The phone number (312) 357-6665... Try their Slinders, min burger with American cheese & pickles served with fries $9... Monk's Chili a cup $4 or bowl $5...Try their grilled cheese and it will melt in your mouth believe you me. I already have been to Monk's... Grill cheese $8.

****

Special note: prices and menu's changed at times. Give these restaurant fair hand shake and you will each of these restaurant cleaned....10 across the board for all them.

THE COUNTY BAR

By Fred Colantonio

The Prime Bar, located at 155 N. Wacker Drive in Chicago, has daily and weekly specials. They have sliders - served on toasted min-buns with fried onion strings - prime rib $9.99 ***** hamburger lettuce, tomato, red onion, pickles, pretzel bun $9.99 w/cheese $10.99 **** California chicken guacamole, shredded romaine, plum tomatoes, julienne cucumbers, fantina cheese, whole wheat kaiser roll $10.99. Give them call at 1.312.884.0000. Ask for Melissa Santiago the General Manager. www.restaurant-america.com

****

Buddy's Guy Legends, 700 S.Wabash Ave. in Chicago, has live blue nightly. Check the groups out. They have lunch special like Southern Fried Okra served basket of okra with hone-mustard sauce for $6.00 ***** Fried Oysters basket of cornmeal breaded oysters served with Cajun cocktail sauce for only $10.00 ***** Highway 61 Caesar Salad romaine lettuce with cherry tomatoes, red onions, caesar dressing, cornbread croutons, and parmesan cheese - Small $5.00 & Large $8.00 - Desert special **** Key Lime Pie $6.00

****

The Burger Joint Chicago, 675 N. Franklin in Chicago, check out the #2 Gyros with cucumber sauce, tomato, onion for a regular size for only $8.99 and a large for $9.99.........Also, #6 Polish with grilled onions and mustard for a regular size for $6.99 and a large for $7.99...They have vanilla, chocolate and strawberry milkshakes for $2.99...Stop in and see Denny for more details. Call 312.440.8600

****

The Moher Public House, 5310 W. Devon Ave. in Chicago, have weekly specials dine only. On Monday's, $5.00 Moher Burger with purchase of a beverage - extra $1.00 - substitutions: $1.00 and on Tuesday's, try $5.00 Well Martinis * $7.00 your call, $1.00 off all drafts and $5.00 quesadilla and finally, Wednesday's half-price bottles of wine $2.00 off flatbreads. Call the Moher Public House at 1.773.467.1954

****

If you would like to make a reservation to any the places we mention, give them call at their phone number today.

CHICAGO SPORTS JOURNAL

AT YOUR SERVICE

The Chocolate Shoppe Ice Cream Store, 5337 W. Devon Ave in Chicago as excellent choices of all kinds of ice cream, milk shakes and sodas as well. They have variety of ice cream cakes made also. Stop in and see Cheryl or Ronnie for more details. The phone number is 1.773.763.9778

****

Trading Post Tobacco & Cigars, 5510 W. Devon Ave in Chicago as fine selection of cigars for your choice and also they have the Illinois State Lottery tickets you can buy. Check out their super website. You will like it. www.tradingpostcigars.com.

****

The Tech Edge, 5355 W. Devon Ave in Chicago will give you a free initial diagnostic & estimate on your computer or laptop. They fast repair turn-around times. Also, web design, computer tutoring and a lot more. Check out their website at www.ttedge.net today.

****

Nico Construction & Remodeling, Inc. does commercial and residential roofing. They are licensed, bonded and insured. Small home repairs made affordable also. Roofing Lic. #104.016095.

****

Glad Cleaners, Inc., 6412 N. Central Ave in Chicago-everything cleaned on premises - same day service. Curtain/Drapery Cleaning, Tailoring & Alterations and Leather Cleaning as well. Stop in Robert Matievic today.

CHICAGO SPORTS JOURNAL

AT YOUR SERVICE

For all your insurance needs from car to home insurance, stop in at Egan and Vance Insurance Agency at 5300 W. Devon Ave in Chicago. Talk to a customer service rep, Coleen M. Egan, CIC or Frank Vance at 1.773.775.0795 or fax them at 1.773.775.0721. Check out their website at http://www.eganvance.com/

****

Media Sound Recording Studio, 6400 N. Leoti Ave in Chicago, offers professional recording services for artists and full bands. This is also includes professional business people'as well. They can transfer analog (LP Vinyl, cassettes) to digital (CD) transfers. Transfer movies from Video 8, VHS, MiniDV, Multisystem PALSECAM, NTSC to DVD.

For more information, give them a call at 1.773.405.3190, ask for Andy. Check out their website at http://www.mediasoundchicago.wordpress.com/ and email at mediasoundchicago@gmail.com.

****

Franklin Newsstand, 225 Wacker Drive, Chicago - offers snacks, sodas, bottle of water, magazines, newspapers, greeting cards and Illinois Lottery tickets as well. They are open Monday thru Friday from 7am to 5pm. Closed on Saturday and Sunday. They are located at the corner of Wacker Drive and Franklin Street.

AT YOUR SERVICE

****

For all your office supply needs, stop in at Atlas Stationers, Inc., 227 W. Lake Street in Chicago. They have excellent selection of stationary, pens, pencils, calendars, office chairs and a lot more. Give them a call at (312) 726.5261 and (312) 726.1069 fax number. Service that makes a world of difference.

****

Let us wash, dry & fold your laundry at $1.45 per lb (10 lbs minimum). This includes shorts, t-shirts - pajamas - socks - hanks - pants - towels - bedhseets - rugs (bathroom) and shower liners. Stop in at Glad Cleaners, 6412 N. Central Ave in Chicago. Call them at 1.773.631.1800 today. http://www.gladcleaners.com/

****

Stop in at 2001 service station located at the corner of Central Ave and Caldwell Ave on the northwest corner in Chicago. Get your gasoline, lottery tickets, newspapers, coffee, snacks, supplies and more.

****

Check out the latest cigar specials at the Trading Post Tobacco & Cigars. They located at 5610 W. Devon Ave in Chicago. Their phone number is 1.773.763.8937 and their website is http://www.tradingpostcigars.com/

AT YOUR SERVICE

Trading Post Tobacco & Cigars, 5510 W. Devon Ave in Chicago as fine selection of cigars for your choice and also they have Illinois Lottery tickets you can buy. They have a special going on. Buy three cigars and get one free in the house cigars. Stop in and see William Espinosa and Tomi Kammer today. Check out their website at www.tradingposttobacco&cigars.com

****

Amlin T.V. Video Sales & Service, located at 8532 W. Lawrence Ave in Norridge, Illinois has outstanding service. They repair Panasonic, Sony, Samsung,

LG, Philips, Sanyo and Vizio. Give them a call at 1.708.452.7487. Check out their website at www.amlintvsalesandrepair.com.

****

Media Sound Recording Studio offers professional recording services for solo artists or full band. Group lessons: one month 4 one hour lessons - $90,00 per person. Two months 8 one hour lessons - $160.00 per person per person.

For more information, contact Andy at 773-405-3190

AT YOUR SERVICE

Trading Post Tobacco & Cigars, 5510 W. Devon Ave in Chicago, as fine selection of cigars for your choice and also they have Illinois Lottery Tickets you can purchase also. They have a daily special - buy any two cigars and get a house cigars FREE! Stop in, see Tommy Kammer and William Espinoisa today. Check out their website www.tradingposttobacco&cigars.com .

****

The Chocolate Ice Cream Store, 5337 W. Devon Ave in Chicago has Mini-gift that serves 2-4 for $15.09; Pie that serves between 6-8 for $20.63; Fudge Nut that serves between 8-12 for only $30.41 - this includes extra deco. All these specials are (All Ice Cream).....For more information, call them at 1.773.763.9778.

Glad Cleaners dry cleaning 20% off order. 20% off with cash payment only. Stop in at Glad Cleaners, 6412 N. Central Ave, Chicago (across from Happy Foods). this off expires on October 31, 2013. For more details, call Glad Cleaners at 1.773.631.1800.

****

Civic Opera Barber Shop, 20 N. Wacker Drive, Chicago - Suite 1549......*Hair Styling for Men, *Conventional Barbering, *Shaving, *Shoe Shine and Manicures. Haircuts $25.00; Haircut Style NG $30.00; Shampoo $10.00; Beards trim $25.00; Shave $30.00; Shoe Shine $4.00; Manicures $12.00.

****

****

The Trading Post Tobacco and Cigars has a variety of new line of cigars from drew estate. Check out Liga Privada Cigars, Norteno Cigars, Undercrown cigars as well. Gift cards are available also. They t-shirts of Trading Post Tobacco and Cigars available for $10.00 also. Hand rolled Puerto Rican Cigars that are rum and sugar cane, cinnamon cigars available as well. Stop in and see Tommy and Bill for anything you need. http://www.tradingpostcigar.com./ Trading Post Tobacco & Cigars, 5510 W. Devon Ave., Chicago IL

****

For all your office supply needs, stop in Atlas Stationers, Inc., 227 W. Lake Street in Chicago. They have excellent selection of stationary, pens, pencils, calendars, office chairs and a lot more. Give them a call at (312) 726-5261 and (312) 726-1069 fax number. Service that makes a world of difference.

****

Civic Opera Barber Shop, located 20 N. Wacker Drive Suite 1549 in Chicago.....They are open Mon-Fri 7am to 5pm and the phone number is 1.312.263.1091.....They offer basic haircuts, head shaves, beard trims, basic neck shaves, hot-lather shaves, moustache trims, manicures, sideburn trims, boot and shoe shines and a lot more. check out their website at www.civicoperabarbershop.com.

****

Stew Cohen, formerly with WYEN (FM) radio in Des Plaines, Illinois published is book called "The WYEN Experience." The Book is awesome to read about the radio station when it got started and a lot more. Pick up a copy today.

By *Fred Colantonio*

Check out the latest at **Glad Cleaners**. They are workers and there is a special going on right now. Let us wash, dry & fold your laundry at $1.45 per lb (10lbs minimum). This includes shorts, t-shirts - pajamas - socks - hanks - pants - towels - bedheets - rug (bathroom) and shower liners.

Stop in at Glad Cleaners, 6412 N. Central Ave in Chicago. Call them at (773) 631-1800 today. http://www.gladcleaners.com/

****

In the Nation, we play favorites... Instead of one company for auto protection, another for home and another for life, you can just go with the one that offers the protection you need. Where you can save up to 25%, just for trusting one company to help protect all the thing you love. We put members first, because we don't have shareholders. Join the Nation one-step shoppers.

Join Carmen Pignatiello
Carmen Pignatiello Agency (630) 800-8254
pignaci@nationwide.com   nationwide.com/pignatiello
12416 S. Harlem Avenue Ste. 101
Palos Heights, Illinois 60463 (708) 923-1600

****

UPS Store, 301 W. Grand Ave in Chicago and you can give them call at (312) 828-0505. Stop in and get all your shipping and mailing service needs. They offer a variety of service for your one-stop solution, including mailbox, printing, mailing, packing, shipping and more outstanding service. They in awesome area of River North of Chicago at the corner of Grand and Franklin. Hours from Mon-Fri 7am to 9pm; Sat 8:30 am to 5:30 pm and Sun 10 am to 4 pm. Stop in and say hello to everyone and George. www.theupsstorelocal.com.

AT YOUR SERVICE

Franklin Newsstand, 225 Wacker Drive, Chicago - offers snacks, sodas, bottle of water, magazines, newspapers, greeting cards and Illinois Lottery as well. They are open Monday thru Friday from 7am to 5pm. Closed on Saturday and Sunday. They are located at the corner of Franklin Street and Wacker Drive.

****

For all your office supply needs, stop in at Atlas Stationers, Inc., 227 W. Lake Street, Chicago. They have excellent selection of stationary, pens, pencils, calendars, office chairs and a lot more. Give them a call at (312) 726.5261 and (312) 726,1069 fax number. Service that makes a world of difference.

****

Penny Pinchers Resale Shop at 4804 N. Central Ave in Chicago, has items that you are interested in - from chairs to furniture. Also, dvds and cds as well. They has have tools, radios, fans and variety to choose from. Give them a call at (773) 545.6666. http://www.pennypinchersresale.net/.

CHICAGO SPORTS JOURNAL

CHICAGO SPORTS JOURNAL

THE RECIPE SHOP

Enchiladas

1-2 lbs of hamburger
1 small onion chopped up
1/2 to 1 tsp of crushed garlic
1 can refried beans
1 can refried beans
1/2 cup of catsup
1 can tomato soup
Mexican cheese

Combine the onion and garlic in a good sized frying pan until somewhat softened, fork in hamburger until the meat is browned (putting the lid on the frying pan hastens the cooking the meat). When meat is ready add refried beans to the mix and combine thoroughly. On the side mix enchilada sauce with catsup and soup. In an oblong pyrex bowl spoon a 1/4 cup of the sauce. Using an 8 to 10 inch soft tortilla shells spoon the meat mixture in each individually roll it up, and place it in the pyrex bowl. Cover the tortillas with the rest of the sauce, and liberally spread packaged Mexican cheese over the tortillas. Place in all in the oven until the cheese begins to bubble up and gets slightly brown it.

— Mr. Joe Gatto, South Bend, Indiana

Beef Skillet Stroganov

1 tablespoon of olive oil
1 lb. of ground beef round steak
1 medium onion chopped
1 can of mushrooms sliced
1 can of Campbell's cream of mushroom soup
1 can of beef broth (college inn)
1 can of sour cream (luse light)

In a skillet brown beef and onion until tender. Blend in other ingredients except sour cream. When it comes to a boil reduce heat, add sour cream and simmer for 10 minutes. Serve with 3 cups of cooked noodles.

— Mrs. Rosemary Turner, Sarasota, Florida

****

THE RECIPE SHOP

Whipped Cream Pound Cake
3 cups all-purpose flour
3 cups sugar
6 large eggs
1 cup whipping cream
1 1/2 teaspoon vanilla extract

Heat oven to 325 degrees, grease a 10 inch tube pen. Sift flour and set aside. Beat butter in a large bowl with an electric mixer on high. Add sugar and continue to beat until mixture is light and fluffy (5 minutes). Add the eggs at a time, mixing well combine cream and vanilla. Alternately add the cream mixture and flour to the batter, mix to combine. Transfer to prepared pan. Smooth with a spatula. Bake until toothpick comes out clean. Bake 80 minutes until a toothpick comes out clean. Cool completely before serving. Yield 18 slices.

- Dolores Gentile, Chicago, Illinois

****

Chicken and Green Beans with Tomato Sauce
1 Chicken, Cut up
3 T olive oil
1 1/2 c chopped onion
1 can Tomato puree or 2 cans tomatoes, diced and one can tomato sauce
1 lb green beans
Salt and pepper to taste
1 stick cinnamon
4 cloves
2 bay leaves

Brown onions and chicken until golden brown. Add beans, tomatoes and spices. Simmer until beans and chicken are cooked through.

- Ramona Zentefis, Des Plaines, Illinois

Vol. XV, No. 3	St. Benedict High School	November 3, 1965

Scope

Published every three weeks by the students of St. Benedict High School.

3900 Leavitt

Chicago, Illinois 60618

Editor-in-Chief Mary Lou Granquist

Asst. Editor _____ Karen Kapolnek

News Editor _____ Pris Bianchini

Writers: Sherry Blaha, Nancy Dietz, Lynn Kotler, Judy Kunz, and Nancy Schneier

Feature Editor _____ Rich Plotzke

Writers: Frances Dekreon, Dennis Ford, Mary Schmidt, Lois Stamper, and Peter Stewart

Exchange Editor _____ Tina Scan

Sports Editor _____ Don Pietschmann

Writers: Fred Colantonio, Bruce Moersch, Frank VanDenBosch, and John Wolf

Typing Co-ordinator ___ Anita Fishik

Typists: Mary Ann Cole, Christine Evangi, Nancy Farrell, and Christine Stegmaier

Moderator _____ Mr. James Rodney

New Sport At St. Ben's Gym Hockey

By Fred Colantonio

Here is the schedule of Intramural games to be played this year at St. Ben's. Coach Golan has again planned a wonderful schedule topped off by adding a new intramural sport, Gym Hockey. It is played on the same order as ice hockey except it has an eight man team, it is played with a plastic stick and a plastic puck and is played on the gym floor instead of on ice. It seems to be a fun sport and we hope to see many of our Bobby Hulls joining it.

Intramural Sports	Begins	Compl. Begins
Table Tennis—S.E.	10/27-9	11/2
Free Throw Con.	11/16-9	11/22
Basketball—D.E.	12/13-7	1/5
Gym Hockey—D.E.	1/26-28	2/7
Volleyball—D.E.	3/ 2-4	3/10
Badminton—S.E.	4/ 5-8	4/12
Tennis—S.E.	4/26-9	5/2

48

Varsity Shoots For Trophy

The interscholastic games that have in the past been played at A.G.O. will this year be played at St. Ben's. This tournament will consist of eight schools of which St. Ben's is one.

The varsity have won it the last two years in a row and if they win this year the traveling trophy will be kept permanently.

The tournament will start on December 7 and last until December 10. It will be a one game elimination.

Coach is making a prediction that even though we don't have height, the players will really put forth a great amount of spirit, effort, and sportsmanship. We will have many more spectators this year than we have had in the past years at St. Ben's. Coach says he is using his E.S.P. and HE KNOWS.

Rumors say possibly something big is going to happen in the Athletic De-partment. In the next few weeks—maybe the boys and girls will be in intramurals together, or maybe there will be mixed gym classes. What is your guess? Whatever it may be, get ready for something unusual and spectacular.

The horseshoe tournament ought to bring some surprises too, because since there are only two boys that have signed up for the Junior-Senior di-vision the first game will be played for the Junior-Senior championship. The Freshmen and Sophomores will com-pete for the frosh-soph championship so the season will be lengthened to more than two games.

If you go by the gym these days after three o'clock you will hear the basketball team practicing.

They're going for the big prize again this year.

Track Team Takes Championship

As the Track season came to a close, we find Saint Benedict's track team the victors once again. Out of the events this year St. Ben's received points for seven of them, giving them a total of 41 points out of a possible 84. For the 100 yard dash Tom Mc-Guire took first and Mike Komos came in second. In the 220 yard dash, Tom and Mike came in second and third. In the 440 yard dash R. Kezele took third place. Dave Fahey, George Keehn and John Moore took first, sec-ond, and third place in that order for the 880 yard dash. Tom McGuire, Mike Komos, R. Kezele, and Jack Bernard came in first place for the 880 yard relay. Mike Groener came in second place for the high-jump.

In the shot put, Wayne Lemke and Don Desimon took first and second. The school is proud of the time and effort put in by these boys and grateful to Coach Gulan and Father Pitts for their excellent coaching, which made it possible for St. Ben's to win first place.

G.A.A. HAD A "FUN"

Plans For Senior Prom Underway

By Lyn Koller

The Class of '66 is planning ahead for their biggest event of the year—the Class Prom. This year the head of the prom committee is Peter Stewert, the co-chairman is Maureen Donahue. Other members of varied committees are as follows: Bobbie Spears, Martin Surges, Terry Breitenbach, and Frank Buttitta. Miss Uhan, a new addition to St. Ben's, is their moderator. One of the committeemen had this to say about Miss Uhan, "She is really won-derful, she is helpful but yet she is not a dictator."

The committee has worked out a questionnaire and passed it out to the Seniors, it contains such questions as: Are you planning to go to the Prom? Where would you prefer to have the Prom? So far these answers were as such: two-thirds of the Seniors are planning to attend the Prom, and two-third's would like the Prom to be held in a country club in some suburb.

The Committee is already working very hard. There is, however, not much that is very definite. The date is planned for the last weekend of May.

New Sport At St. Ben's Gym Hockey

By Fred Colantonio

Here is the schedule of Intramural games to be played this year at St. Ben's. Coach Gulan has again planned a wonderful schedule topped off by adding a new intramural sport, Gym Hockey. It is played on the same order as ice hockey except it has an eight man team, it is played with a plastic stick and a plastic puck and is played on the gym floor instead of on ice. It seems to be a fun sport and we hope to see many of our Bobby Hulls joining it.

Intramural Sports	Entries Taken	Compet. Begins
Table Tennis—S.E.	10/27-9	11/2
Free Throw Con.	11/16-9	11/22
Basketball—D.E.	12/13-7	1/5

Scope

Published every three weeks by the students of St. Benedict High school.

3900 Leavitt

Chicago, Illinois 60618

Editor-in-Chief   Mary Lou Cranquist

Second Editor .... Karen Kapolnek

News Editor .... Pris Bianchini

Writers: Sherry Blaha, Nancy Dietz, Lynn Koller, Judy Kunz, and Nancy Schaefer

Feature Editor ....Rich Plotzke

Writers: Frances Dekreon, Dennis Ford, Mary Schmidt, Lois Stam-er, and Peter Stewart

Exchange Editor .... Tina Stan

Sports Editor ..... Don Pietschmann

Writers: Fred Colantonio, Bruce Moersch, Frank VanDenBosch, and John Wolf

Typing Co-ordinator .... Anita Fishuk

THIS ISSUE
IS DEDICATED TO
MR. JAMES RODNEY,
SCOPE'S NEW
MODERATOR

Vol. XV, No. 3   **St. Benedict High School**   **November 3, 1965**

New Leaders Get Head Start

"The Junior Party on November 13 will be a gas!" This seems to be the feeling of everything the Junior Class does this year. As the class president, Jim Pilarski, said. "We want to make up for the fun we missed in other years and through that obtain a strong unity within our class."

The first signs of this unity are already shown in the way that the Junior Board members work together.

"By the representation at the Board meetings it is evident that they are willing to work. Also our coordinators have already given us a lot of help. Since this year is an important one, we had better get going."

The Sophomore Class officers are also on the move. They believe they will be able to carry out many plans, because, in the words of Pat Mulhern, class President, "We have a very cooperative class which is very willing to work."

The Vice-President, Nancy Simkowski, has faith in her class. "The

Sodality Holds Party For Under-Privileged Children
by Judy Kunz

"Is that witch real?"

"Can we really keep the puppets?"

These were common queries at the Halloween Party the Sodality gave on October 30 at Martin de Paurs Center. The children were treated to puppet shows, Halloween goodies, and a real live witch.

The children enjoyed themselves immensely and although it was a lot of work, the Sodalists may have had more fun than the kids.

The kids, about thirty six and seven-year olds were the recipients of a Sodality tradition of giving a Halloween Party every year for some needy organization. This experience was entirely different for the Sodalists from the other parties in that the situation was totally different. This gave the Sodalists the opportunity to put brotherhood into action.

This was the first experience of this kind especially for the newly received Sophomore Sodalists. On October 11 they were received in the Sodality by Father Pitts, Sodality Counselor at the Mass and Reception Ceremony held in the chapel after school. This was followed by a small celebration in the cafeteria.

Young leaders gather to plan ideas for 1965-1966 school year.

These reflections by Linda Kirnbaur, class Vice-President, support the fact that the Juniors are on their way.

Tom Mocon, class Treasurer commented, "This will be a great year because there is so much spirit in the Junior Class. Also, we have had our coordinators behind us from the beginning."

To Carol Couch, Class Secretary, unification of the class is "essential to keep the class going. Last year the school did a lot, and we should keep up the spirit."

Carol also believes that "all students

class leaders, especially the president, have good background experience; they know what's going on."

A man behind his president is Rich Kurkes, Class Treasurer. "I like Pat's ideas and with the rest of the officers and class moderators, I know he will work for the advancement of the entire class."

Bringing their ideas down to specifics, the Class Secretary, Lenore Volante, said, "One of the aims of the Sophomore class would be free seating in the cafeteria."

With these people as Junior and Sophomore class officers, this year...

286-6100 & 4943 N. Milwaukee Avenue

Number 16
Volume 12   Week of April 23, 1978   15 CENTS PER COPY
                                                    50 CENTS PER MONTH

sauganash

HANK JOYCE   **sampler**
286-7527

RESIDENTS ALONG the Sauganash area are busy getting their spring cleaning done, working on their yards and front lawn.

* * *

SAUGANASH PARK, 5816 N. Kostner, is having the following programs for children between the ages 8 to 15 years old. Programs start May 1. On Mondays at 4 p.m., Girls track and field for girls 8 to 15 years old.

On Tuesdays at 3:30 p.m., boys track and field; 4:30 p.m., there is softball for boys between the ages 12-14 years old.

On Wednesdays for girls between the ages 13-14, there is softball and starting time is at 4 p.m.

On Thursdays there is softball for boys 12-14 and track and field for boys 8-13. Starting time is 3:30 p.m.

On Fridays there is softball for girls between 10-12 years old.

For more information about sporting events and tournaments at Sauganash Park District, stop by at 5816 N. Kostner or give them a call. All in all, it sounds like it will be a a exciting year.

* * *

SAUGANASH COMMUNITY Church has a new Pastor. His name is Rev. John Jewell. The Sauganash Community Church also has announced that they will have a Rummage sale this Thursday from 10 a.m. until 8 p.m. There will be a lot of bargains on sale at the Church. Everyone is welcome. Stop by and say hello to the new Pastor.

speaker will be Ms. Babias of The Fashion Show. For more details about the Luncheon and Fashion show, contact Mrs. Boyle at 773-5755.

* * *

POLISH NATIONAL Alliance, 6100 N. Cicero, will be in the Downtown Chicago May 3 parade. Rosalynn Carter will be the main speaker. For more information write to PNA or give them a call.

* * *

THE SAUGANASH Community Association will hold its regular monthly meeting on May 15.

* * *

QUEEN OF ALL Saints Sodality will have its annual Spring Luncheon fashion show

51

Frederick Colantonio

PRESS & JOURNAL

286-6100 & 4941 N. Milwaukee Avenue

Number 15
Volume 12

Week of April 9, 1978

CENTS PER COPY
CENTS PER MONTH

Week of April 9, 1978 — Page 13

sauganash sampler

HANK JOYCE
286-7527

A COMMITTEE OF PARENTS from Sauganash Elementary School are trying real hard to have the school painted and repaired.

The committee was formed last year. Members of the Sauganash School Parents and Maintenance Committee are as follows: Frederic M. Rizzo, chairman; other members include Frank and Eleanor Pascher; Kenneth Ditkowsky, Ed Galassini, Bud Hodgkinson, Teresa Merrifield, Nancy Jakob, Alan and Ann Johnson, Jerry and Marcia Janis, San and Patti Maloria.

The needs for the school are as follows: 1) plaster; 2) interior paint; 4) walls; 5) lighting; 6) lockers; 7) sidewalks and much more work.

The committee would like to see the school roof replaced and window shades for the inside of the school. The school is in need of your help.

* * *

THE SAUGANASH PARK and Fieldhouse are still closed due to the construction work. Hopefully the park will open between 3-4 weeks.

* * *

IF YOU LOVE Bingo, then you want to stop over at Billy Caldwell Post, 6033 N. Cicero Ave. every Thursday night at 7:30 p.m. The... twenty-one prizes... $20 to $500. You will really enjoy yourself very much.

SAUGANASH Community Church Guild is in need of shirts, sheets, towels and blankets. You can drop things off every second and fourth Wednesdays of the months from 10 a.m. to 2 p.m. If you are interested in joining their group or dropping off any of the items, please phone AV 3-3847 for details.

* * *

A SPECIAL HELLO to, Mr. and Mrs. Stanley Wojnicki, 6343 N. Tripp Ave. Mr. Wojnicki is with the Chicago Fire Prevention Bureau on Eastwood Ave.

* * *

IF YOUR GROUP, church or school has any announcements to be made in this column or newspaper, write to: Press-Reporter- Journal, 4941 N. Milwaukee Ave. Chicago 60630, or phone 286-7527 after 5 p.m.

52

The Sauganash Sounds

Vol. 15, No. 4   6030 N. Hiawatha, Chicago, Il. 60646   777-3337   November 9.

Serving Sauganash, Sauganash Park, Edgebrook, Wildwood, Lincolnwood Towers and Sauganash Village Communities

RESTAURANT REVIEW

FOOD FAX BAKERY & CAFE
4748 W. PETERSON
CHICAGO, IL
PHONE (312) 202-9750

FOOD FAX, near the corner of Cicero on Peterson, offers a wide selection of taste tempting treats, from old-fashioned cinnamon rolls and sticky buns, to exquisitely prepared cakes and tortes.

The cafe, although limited in seating, is charming with decor of mostly hand-crafted cookie jars, which I was told were all for sale, filled with a variety of butter cookies, starting at $21.95.

During our visit we had a chance to partake of some of the selections from their menu. The Italian style spaghetti, only $3.50, was served piping hot, with a delicious homemade sauce and garlic bread. From their salad selection we chose a seafood salad, $3.75. It was quite refreshing, as it had real crab meat, tiny shrimp, and was garnished with fresh vegetables and lemon wedges. It was served with choice of muffin, which gave us quite a task, as the homemade muffins are baked daily and the variety is quite numerous.

In choosing a dessert, we tried a chocolate eclair, $1.50 and an apple square, 85¢. Both were a delicious conclusion to our luncheon.

Before leaving, I though it

by Hank Joyce

would be a nice treat for my family, to take something home. I chose the turtle torte, $7.95, an 8-inch chocolate cake filled with chocolate fudge, caramel, and pecans—"Excellent."

FOOD FAX, I believe, will be a welcome addition to the Sauganash-Edgebrook neighborhood—especially with the holiday season coming.

Store Hours—Monday thru Friday 6 AM to 7 PM; Saturday and Sunday 8 AM to 4 PM.

CLOSING REMARKS

My journey of visiting the nation's baseball and hockey teams has not ended. I will be reporting my visits in my quarterly newspaper, CHICAGO SPORTS JOURNAL, as the opportunity presents itself.

Printed in the United States
By Bookmasters